Day and Night

Night

The 21st Century Work Environment

Candice Waldo

ARGYLE FOX
PUBLISHING

For my parents

Introduction

Through my own work experience, my awareness
of social justice concerns heightened—namely
the injustices and discriminatory practices in the
American workplace.

My poetry reflects this reality, describing the trials
and tribulations of the modern work environment
from a unique and interesting perspective. It explores
the differences and challenges people face in the
workplace.

I suspect you will find something to relate to in these
pages, and I hope one day such realities will be left in
the past.

Hoops

Fiery hoops of fire encased in golden picture frames.
Feet treading on hot black coals invisible to the naked eye.
Noisy, heeled shoes stomping in the hallway,
Marching to an airy office space.

Power throughout the floor—
Sweating bullets at the meeting table,
Shooting daggers during a presentation,
Mirror, mirror on the wall, who's the toughest of them all?

Cooling off with beads of icy water in the receptacle.
All in a day's work, walking through another hoop.

Is This It?

My everyday experience as an educated female in society—
Morning, noon, and night to no avail,
Subjected to demeaning behavior
In and out of the workplace—
Degrading and, yes, thoughtless comments socially
With financial concerns looming, though
Focusing on the bigger picture: financial security.

To take an exit from the workforce sooner than later,
Because if this is it, then it's not for someone like me:
Ambitious and educated.

For now, to fight the good fight somewhere else,
Where my efforts are appreciated and—
      Let's face it—well compensated.

Challenging Dreams

Achieving one's career goals is not easy,
Especially as a woman of color; throughout society,
Encountering obstacles from friends and foes alike,
Yet adhering to the adage that "Tough times do not last long,"
And so staying resilient and motivated
Because I truly understand that
I have positioned myself for the best
That life has to offer, professionally and otherwise.

Unjust

Pandemic work and life upends everything,
Daily indignities heightened during the pandemic crisis,
Social inequities prevalent even more throughout society.
Being a person of color in and out of the workplace
Can be a challenge;
Yet, I am here for the challenge and transformational process.

The duality of gender and racial discrimination
Forces one to exercise resilience, persistence, and perseverance
        rather quickly
In order to meet life's challenges and effectively encounter
        obstacles—
Efforts and attempts to erase one's history, contributions,
        and rights.

So, no, the fight is not over against unjust actions.

Workweek Warfare

Combative workplace behavior from others,
Hostile enemies outnumbering affable coworkers in a
professional work setting,
Casualties of pink slips, demotions, and terminations—
An office that is undeniably a battlefield.
So many barriers, challenges, and obstacles
Toward the pursuit of career glory.

Walking on Eggshells

Two-inch kitten heels
Prancing the four corners of a windowless room.
Another small victory
Quietly kept to oneself.
Delicately using one's words
To avoid further confrontation and
Unwanted attention.
Another email message sent and
Masterfully crafted and
Purposefully ignored.

High Hopes

Having high hopes
Of fulfilling my dreams and career aspirations,
I make concerted efforts to achieve those dreams and goals
In order for them to come into fruition.
Not expecting the impossible.
Rather, motivated and confident of the best to come,
      career-wise.

Special

Sitting at my desk at the office,
Ready to take on the world
And all of its challenges.
Swiveling from side to side in my chair,
While reviewing document files
And scrolling news-related websites.
A much-needed reprieve from the cruelties of the world,
Where I face
Unfathomable discrimination in and out of the workplace.

Pep in My Step

Healthy smoothies,
All abroad—
Ready, set, go!
Eyes glued to the projector screen,
Fingers gently tapping the surface
Of a soft, ironed cloth
Adorned with finger bowls of candy—
Little rays of sunshine,
Chewed softly,
While listening to the management guru.

A New Start

The privilege of thriving in one's career
Is a rarity for most women of color
Despite impressive credentials and excellent qualifications.
Acknowledging an unequal playing field and dichotomy
between the genders
But focusing onward,
On continuously elevating one's life.

Unfinished Business

In the boardroom
Or in the courtroom—
In any given work setting,
Executing brilliance and excellence among the unassuming,
Becoming an amazingly cultivated professional
Within the world where there is always unfinished business.

Showtime

Lights, camera, action!
All eyes are on me
To educate and persuade
Persons of influence,
Pillars of society,
Into advancing my cause
For the greater good—
Or at least for those who cannot help themselves.

Delicioso

Wholesome food, prepared with tender loving care.
Satisfaction guaranteed.
Let's chat
Over a warm cup of soup.
A calm before the storm.
Ah, celery sticks!
Do you want cheese with that?
I surely do, and
Some of that bread and butter, too.
Yes, sir—the whole enchilada.

Just Another Day

Eager to make it,
Highly motivated to do hard work and persevere
Despite systemic barriers and inequalities
Within the workplace,
All to achieve career success and fulfillment.
Be gone, unconscious bias and
        implicit discriminatory practices!

Just another day to experience sexism and racism
And just another day to combat it.

Silk

Intricate patterns
Drawn out as graphs.
Meticulously thought-out memos
Prepared carefully and
Read by many eyes,
Information delivered smoothly on the silver screen.
Like the silk blouse worn by the newscaster.
Now, I'll take that coffee with cream.

Taking Care of Business

It's all a juggling act.

Tsk, task.

Ah, where is my cape?
Along with the accolades.

Push come to shove,
Business will be taken care of.

Life Right Now

Experiencing endless discrimination and
      sometimes harassment,
Enduring bull crap in and out of the workplace,
Seeking a more ideal work environment,
Giving zero cares to ignorant naysayers.

Believing in one's self, skills, and abilities
For a much better life experience.

A Networker

Who, me?!
Why yes, I am a networker (out of necessity).
Networking toward my career goals
Of achieving greatness/goodness in the workplace.
My best self-advocate for meaningful career opportunities.

It goes without saying that I continue to expand my network
Because at some point, it's who you know.

Fast

My life changed so fast—
With the click of a mouse,
No acceptance speech necessary.

My resignation is official.

This prima donna is out the revolving door, and
Life goes on as it certainly does.

This day could not end any quicker.
Tick, tock.

The tension is transparent.
Sighs of relief,
But I'm on to the next opportunity,
Which cannot come quickly enough.

Climbing

Are you a social climber?

Um no, you pompous jerk.
I climb to get a fantastic workout,
A form of relief from it all—
Striving for Zen amidst the chaos,
Exercising to sustain greatness.
Care to join me on a climbing adventure?

Breathing Room

This corner office
Is coveted.
The cubicles outside of it
Are not—
Unless you expect less in the working world
Or have lofty goals and proceed to the nearest exit
To set up shop elsewhere.

Over It

Despite having relevant work experience,
Being a graduate of an elite college,
And having an advanced degree,
I am, once again, deemed too inexperienced,
Too old for an ideal career opportunity.

At this moment,
I am through with the job search process in America,
Over with the excuses to not advance in the workplace.

Humor Me

What's up?
Spell insubordination.
Loosen up!
Spell termination.

Believe it or not,
I've been out in the trenches for nearly twenty years.

I repeat...
I. AM. NOT. YOUR. PEER.

Pack your ish
While listening to Pandora.

The Country

Bales of hay,
Long country roads,
Police at every corner
During the excursion into the country.

Excursion?
More like a death sentence.
Trekking into the unknown, the unfamiliar terrain
To reach my destination,
Complete another assignment.

Another day, another place, another jerk
Awaiting to torture another person
Living in anguish
Just trying to survive the workplace.

Godiva: An Homage to My Candy Provider

Only the best—
A sampler or various assortment of candies—
Will not do for Boss's Day.
You help provide food for that table
Purchased at IKEA, no less.
Clothes on my back
Provided courtesy of the GAP.
And equally important, shelter,
That loft within walking distance of my favorite haunts.
This candy,
It's the least I could do.

Working Life

Started as an intern while an undergraduate
Then a newly minted college graduate,
Subsequently having a working life
Dismayed with a lack of suitable career opportunities,
Prompting an inevitable return to school—
      professional school, law school—
In order to be a more viable candidate in the workforce.
Armed with a law degree
And yet facing resistance
  in the pursuit
  of more meaningful
  career opportunities
  here in America.

LAW

Foot Solider

This working woman
Wearing kitten heels—thank you—
Hits the pavement every day,
Down the street
On the sidewalk
To a place where words cut like a knife.
In some circles, she is not brave,
Just another working stiff
Trying to survive another day in the concrete jungle.

At Ten

At ten—
You, clock watcher you, looking at that digital clock, or
You being time conscious ends a chat over the coffee maker
To tie up loose ends, so to speak, or
You, boss man, what are you up to? or
You, boss lady, reapplying your war paint or lipstick,
Eye your subordinate who needs to be told a thing or two.

As usual, at ten o'clock in the morning,
Where are you?
At the gym or
On the golf course or
Working on your backhand at the tennis court.
Lucky you.
At ten, I'm here. To stay.
Or at least until I'm no longer needed.
However that is defined.
Hey, at ten I'm doing okay.

Welcome Back

Or should I say
Go to the nearest exit,
Because you are unwelcome. Unwanted.

Suspicions abound.

Who do you think you are—
A superstar?

Amuse me,
Because I will amuse you
With my antics, my immaturity.
Not a chance.

Shadow

Join me.
Immerse yourself.
Isn't this engaging?
My work, that is.
Sustains me.
Fulfills me.

The Champ

You've overcome many obstacles
To reach this zenith,
This pinnacle of success.
You moved effortlessly through metaphorical hoops,
Dancing around a detour here and there
On the road to success,
A journey, no less.

Lessons learned.
Mistakes made from time to time.

Shedding a few tears.
Taking a hit, a blow.
Enduring hard times.
Yet making it out of hellish periods like a champ.

Numbers

It's a number game.
As they say, numbers don't lie.
Check the spreadsheet.
Make sense? No!
Well, it ought to.
Look at it carefully.
Am I missing something
Or are you?

Angel

Were you sent from the heavens
To help me grow this business?
Because I think you were.
You're an angel—
To me at least.
Stay here,
Work here.
Indefinitely.

Angel II

Come in early,
Leave late,
Brews pots of coffee,
Keeps the supply closet stocked with goodies
(Like my beloved sticky notes).
Always pleasant with a welcoming smile—
That's an angel.

Moving On

I'm moving on.
Oh yeah, to where?
Wouldn't you like to know!
She ain't going nowhere.
Oh, sis, that girl is going places.

I.T.

You are vain.
I can do this better all by myself—
Fixing this computer.
You heartless jerk, I've got a job to do
And FYI,
Lose the attitude.
On that note, good morning and goodbye.
Close the door behind you.

Water Cooler

I see you.
You see me.
Posing at the water cooler.
Getting the latest and the greatest.
Now back to the grindstone.

Water Cooler II

It's getting tense in here.
So many dynamics at play.
Where do I begin?
Where else, but at the water cooler.
Diffuse the tension
With a few sips of H_2O.

Unwanted

Story of my life,
From place to place.
Considered dispensable,
By society at least.
Got to keep shining
For my family's sake.

Unwanted II

Unwanted.
Underpaid.
Dispensable.

Get the picture?

Day and Night

Toiling away
Day and night,
For what?
To store away some coins
For my future.

Day and Night II

Rise and shine, sweetheart
It's just another day in the workplace.
Type this, Listen to me!
Ugh, some people are so demanding.
Other folks, so taxing.

Let's meet again
For the umpteenth time.
Don't you know I have actual work to complete?
And ironically, it's all for you,
Which you gotta have in a certain time frame.

I bid you farewell,
See you in the morning.
Have a good one.
Get some sleep,
Cause you're one of America's most productive worker bees.

Good Work

Was it good for you?
Ah, I didn't think so.
Oh well,
Another missed opportunity.

Good Work II

Too good for this place,
Yet underpaid.
Are you familiar with pay equity?
Don't pretend to be.
I'm over it—this bull crap.

I'm outta here.

Corporate Supply Chain

Who's in charge here?
Oh, you don't know?
You've haven't been given the lay of the land, eh?
Not yet.

Snakes

Them backstabbers,
Immoral beings,
Two-faced snakes—
They're all alike:
Full of ambiguity.

Prize

What prize?
I've lost sight of it.
Temporarily.
Discouraged yet not undeterred
From finding a path to success.

Wires Crossed

Didn't mean to offend.

Oh, you didn't?
Could have fooled me.

Welcome to the Barrel

No, we're not talking about the infamous restaurant
And old country store
But the tiny crustaceans that metaphorically
Try to climb out of a barrel.

Upward mobility, you say,
"You better get in where you fit in!"

Oh, and where is that?

War Paint

Smears of paint,
Lipstick on my cheek
From another round.
And the final verbal blow
Directed from a colleague.
Me, begrudgingly holding back tears.

Nameless

You.
Yeah, you!
Come over here.
Work on this.
Do this.
Do that.
By the end of the day
You'll end up with nothing.

Nothing is nameless,
A nameless nobody for now.

Whipping Board

Ticktock,
And I don't stop
Until I become your whipping board.

Scrutiny

All eyes are on me.

That is all
For now.

The Groomer

Groomed for excellence,
I tell ya!
Lucky you.
Fortunate enough to have a groomer.

The Horizon

Let's fight the war,
Overcome our fears,
Prepare for battle.
Stay up...please!

The Hit

Paperwork piling up every which way.
Where do I start?

Seems endless.

Well, at least there's work to be completed.
Hit after hit.

Good Stuff

On the prowl
For the good stuff.
Can't live
Without my sticky notes.

The Best of Me

Every day you get the best of me.
Every day you take my work for granted.
Every day
It's a battle at this place.
Every day I think about moving on.

Brothers and Sisters

Some are brotherly,
Some not so much.
Some are sisterly,
Some not so much.

Those who are,
They're superstars.

Soft

How can something so soft
Have something so harsh written on it?
It distresses me,
Forces me to make major moves—
And quickly!

See Ya

Goodbye and good riddance!
You were never that good.

Oh yeah?!
Somebody thinks so!
See ya!
And not in this work space.

Wild

Honey, you don't like these streaks
Of sunlight in my hair?
Well, you're not quite with it.
My dear, you were left behind
In some other space and time.
Time to live it up—
At least for now,
While you're still oh-so wild.

Happiness

Will this ever be attainable for me
In the workplace
And outside these walls, at home?
Because work makes me happy —
Especially a consistent flow of it.
Tidal wave, though,
And I'm gone.

Oh, Behave

Oh, behave!
But you know you won't—
At least not in front of me.
Cause in your world, I don't matter.
However, in someone else's world,

I am loved.

This is what REALLY matters.
Now, back to you.
You're still a jerk at the end of the day.

Second

Fifteen minutes seems like forever
When your livelihood is at stake.
Or is it?
Will I ever be treated like a first-class citizen?
For now, I am subjected to this madness.

Vacation Mode

Days without end,
Full of tedious and mundane work.

Excited about disconnecting from all electronics, gadgets, and devices,
Embracing rest and relaxation on a temporary basis.
A vacation is certainly welcomed.

Enjoying the vacation experience
Until one returns back to work,
Not feeling the least bit homesick.

Break

Much needed respite
From work.
Here, have another sip
Of this energy smoothie.
Sustenance is needed
To continue one's mission.

Back to Work

Back to work
After giving life to one's greatest accomplishment.
Back to work
After a much-needed vacation.
Back to work
After marrying the love of one's life.
Back to meaningful, fulfilling work.
Back to work that I love
Back to not missing a beat.

Myself V. Myself

No need at all to be at war with myself
When at times it seems as though
Most of the world is against me.
Yet I am determined to be great,
To seek and achieve goodness in this world
No matter what may be.
Why?
Because
I, too,
Deserve all that is good.

It's Yours

It's your job
Claim it at the initial interview
If
You are ready and willing
To do good work.

The Ladder

Hold steady!

Climbing was never easy—
Disappointments and setbacks
Just to join another rank,
Another pathway
Made possible by persistent efforts
To reach the pinnacle of success.

Enamored

With you,
Anything is possible.
Mornings are bearable,
Pleasantries are even sweeter.
Ignoring even the biggest slight,
Because of you.

Before Nine

I've pulled another all-nighter
Tending to my familial brood.
All before nine.
Now it's time to
Go to my other job
To support my growing family
Before and after nine.

One's work is never done.

North of 40

The best is yet to come
Personally and professionally—
Reaching professional goals and
Breaking the mold,
Smashing a glass ceiling,
Overcoming a myriad of obstacles
And defying the naysayers,
All with the ease and confidence of an individual north of 40.

Thursdays

Thursdays could not come any sooner in the week,
Yet still not a Friday!
Thursdays may be a drag—
Still longing for the weekend,
A glimpse of freedom in the near future.
Still past Wednesday's hump,
Yet still not a Friday!

Heaven

Morning greetings are such pleasantries
Followed by a peak of paradise outside the window pane.
Heavenly workspace
Set within elegant confines.

At work,
I finally found a glimpse
Of heaven.

Winter Sky

Beauty is in the snow and frost.
Quietness and solitude are welcomed,
Calmness embraced,
And joy overdue.

The coldness beckons togetherness
Along with rest for the weary
During long and frigid nights,
Work professionals benefiting from the shorter days.

Making the most of wintertime,
Finding reward underneath the winter sky.

Closure

At sunset, there is no closure for the weary.
Still more work
To be completed.
Under the starry sky
Busy bodies abound,
Especially in the ever-growing metropolis.